Mark Hannah

Athens of the North

Salamander Street

PLAYS

First published in 2025 by Salamander Street Ltd., a Wordville imprint. (info@salamanderstreetcom).

Athens of the North Mark Hannah, 2025

Cover image by Robyn Black

Photography inside by Elliot Hetherton

PB ISBN: 9781068233425

10 9 8 7 6 5 4 3 2 1

Further copies of this publication can be purchased from www.salamanderstreet.com

Wordville

Athens of The North is dedicated to the memory of

Edith May Ramsay (née Gargaro)

January 24th 1941 - January 23rd 2020

A child of the Old Town; a ship-steadier, a truth teller.

"I have wasted so much time,

time that was not mine to waste,

and now I cry for that wasted time,

and pull up my soul from the dark cave in which I have

kept it all this while and I say,

you are free."

Ian Charleson, 1989

ACKNOWLEDGEMENTS

With thanks to all those whose help, guidance, inspiration, friendship, promotion and kindness made this production and publication possible...

Fraser Scott, Lucy George at Salamander Street, Kevin Ramsay, The Hibernian Supporters Club, Daniel Abercrombie, The Scottish Storytelling Centre, Leith Theatre, Alistair Maxwell, Jack MacGregor, Kieran Hurley, Cora Bissett, Rory Kinnear, Sarah Milton, Mark Fisher, Brian Ferguson, Gordon Stirling, Jim Slaven, Callum Kane, Bonnie Prince Bob, Ned Bennett, Ross Willis, Harry Gould, Kira Guess, Jack Robertson, Riverside Studios Hammersmith, Iwan Rheon, Dean and Josie Gribble, Emma Cooney, all of my era at the London Academy of Music and Dramatic Art, all of my friends at Leyton Orient Football Club, The Simpsons–22 Short Films About Springfield, my family and of course the people of Edinburgh; of the past, the present and the future.

INTRODUCTION

To write about *Athens of the North* by Mark Hannah, first I really need to write about Edinburgh. And to write about Edinburgh in the way Mark's play demands I do, first I need to write a bit about me. Trust a fellow writer to make it all about themselves.

Edinburgh is many places at once to me. There's the city I grew up in, specifically around the streets of Lochend, Restalrig, Craigentinny, Portobello, Meadowbank and Leith. And there's the city I now return to every year in my professional capacity as a playwright, for the Edinburgh Fringe. There's the city of my childhood, the streets as I remember from the 90s and 2000s. And there's the streets as they are now, the present competing with memory, nostalgia and the impulse to tell my uninterested kids how that bit never used to be like that by the way, and this thing here was never there before at all. All of these Edinburghs overlap and interact, but at the same time, even when they're literally the same place, they're never quite the same place.

That Edinburgh is a city of different shifting sides is not a new idea. It's woven through the literature the city has produced, the stories it has told about itself. It's written into the geography of the place, the history of its foundations, the dividing lines of the subterranean Cowgate and George IV Bridge overhead. For me, it's an experience of the city that's fraught with personal tensions. I love the festivals, and all they've enabled for me, and at the same time it can be hard, when subsumed within the version of Edinburgh they produce, to truly feel a sense of home. Rushing through the city with lanyards round my neck to catch an exciting visiting show from London, before off to other meetings with people who have set up temporary camp in town for a few days, I really am just another transient guest in the international trades fair of my profession. "I'll see you during Edinburgh," I'm told, as if the existence of the place was fleetingly time-limited—which, as far as this version of it is concerned, it sort of is. When, at some point in my 20s, I began to notice that on certain streets, in certain parts of town, memories and experiences of this transient, professional, visitor relationship with the city were beginning to overlay and push out memories of my own adolescence, it was a moment of genuine psychic pain. I would re-walk the streets of the Old Town and around the Meadows, scrambling internally to assert a particular, fading, version of them, of their story and mine, in my mind. These different Edinburghs competing with each other, all the time, even just inside one guy.

Athens of the North is a play that knows these things about Edinburgh. It's a play that feels it, too. In one sense it is a play that sits in a long Scottish tradition of finding beauty in the quiet humanity of ordinary working class lives. Watching Mark perform this play, you can't help but be struck by his intimate connection to and deep affection for the voices that he channels. It's storytelling as love song, to a place, but more importantly to people, and to the types of people that have shaped who the author is. But it is also a quiet act of defiance. It's a play that insists that in the competing noise of different Edinburghs a particular version of the city's truth will be seen, and will be heard. A version rooted in the voices of its local people. Whatever I was doing by re-tracing my steps on those Old Town streets, reaching for and holding on to a particular version of the city, I get the sense that Mark Hannah is doing the same thing in these pages, with paper and with pen.

When I first saw *Athens of the North* it was performed during the Fringe but away from the fray, in the Hibernian Supporters Club—the only Fringe show on in a venue frequented by the same local people it seeks to represent. It demanded then, that I step out of the city centre, and towards the streets I was raised on. This simple act was like an antidote to the frenzy of the festival city. The familiarity of the neighbourhood, the long-standing sense of connection, the accents of the audience chattering before the play starts. Unusually, for this time of year, for this experience of Edinburgh, a sense, for me, of home. For this new run at the Scottish Storytelling Centre, the play takes up residence on the Royal Mile. I believe that Mark's own family history makes this another homecoming of sorts. But it's also heartening to me to know that this play—the Edinburgh that it holds and wants to share with you—will exist right in the heart of festival city.

I hope and expect that this play—and this production—will be seen by many people. I hope it spreads far and wide, that in being published it might be picked up by young actors looking for audition monologues and discovering the thrill of a character who talks like they do. I hope it's picked up by student groups in universities across the lands who struggle badly with the accent, but in doing so build a wee bridge in their minds and their hearts to a perspective beyond theirs. I hope it's translated into multiple languages by people who recognise that the locally and culturally specific always, ultimately, contains the universal. But, more selfishly, I'll always be glad that I got to see it in the Pat Stanton Lounge upstairs in the Hibs club, in a little corner of an Edinburgh I know.

Kieran Hurley

2025

Athens of The North premiered in the Pat Stanton Lounge at the Hibernian Supporters Club as part of the Edinburgh Festival Fringe 2024. This definitive version was published to coincide with a run in the Netherbow Theatre at the Scottish Storytelling Centre at the Edinburgh Festival Fringe 2025.

Writer/Performer: **Mark Hannah**

Director: **Fraser Scott**

Movement Support: **Jack Webb**

THE CAST AND CREATIVES

Mark Hannah | Playwright & Performer

Mark is an actor and playwright who was born in Edinburgh and trained on the BA Acting programme at the London Academy of Music and Dramatic Art during the entirety of the COVID-19 pandemic, graduating in 2022. During his training he played the titular role in *Julius Caesar* as well as appearing in the epic *The LeftOvers* directed by Ned Bennett. Prior to his training, Mark appeared in *GRIT—The Martyn Bennett Story* and *Janis Joplin Full Tilt* both directed by Cora Bissett. More recently, Mark has undertaken numerous voice works for Audible, namely *Bleak House* by Charles Dickens, and also Irvine Welsh's 2025 film *Reality Is Not Enough*. As a playwright, Mark was selected to participate in The Royal Court's Open Court programme in the summer of 2016, where he wrote and performed segments of his work in the Jerwood Upstairs. He was also a member of the Traverse Young Writers as well as performing more of his own work as part of the Making Space programme at Dundee Rep in 2019.

Athens of The North is his debut play.

Fraser Scott | Director

Fraser Scott is a director from Paisley.

Fraser directed *Athens of the North* while studying an MFA in Theatre Directing at Birkbeck University, where he was supported by the Andrew Lloyd Webber Foundation Scholarship and the Cross Trust. From 2024-2025 he was the Resident Assistant Director at the Octagon Theatre, and he graduated from the Royal Conservatoire of Scotland with a BA in Filmmaking in 2020.

Other directing credits include: *The Gray Plays* (Òran Mór), *Common Tongue* (Lanternhouse Cumbernauld), *Godspell* (Drygate) and *CRISIS: A Rallying Cry* (Traverse Theatre).

"*A poignant episodic monologue which celebrates Edinburgh and its people. Hannah embodies three distinct characters, opening with struggling single-parent Alan, driving to St Giles Cathedral. Next is love-struck Liam, in search of his holiday romance. Finally, ageing Maureen reminisces about her past. Each character interacts uniquely with the city, sharing untold stories of ordinary life. Hannah thus explores the complexities and beauty of human nature, using his magic ability to suddenly switch from buoyant banter to raw, dark emotion.*"

Corr Blimey

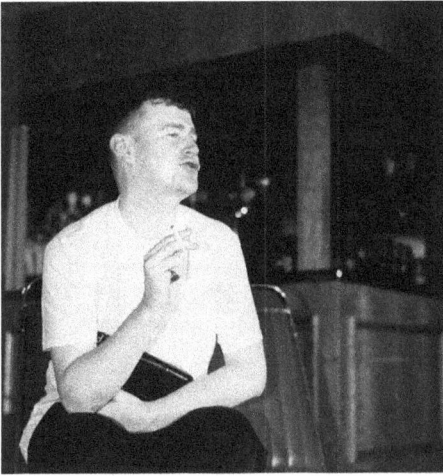

"*Hannah performs three interlinking monologues rich in the culture and place names of the city. Punchily written and powerfully performed, these portraits hold the audience spellbound.*"

The Guardian

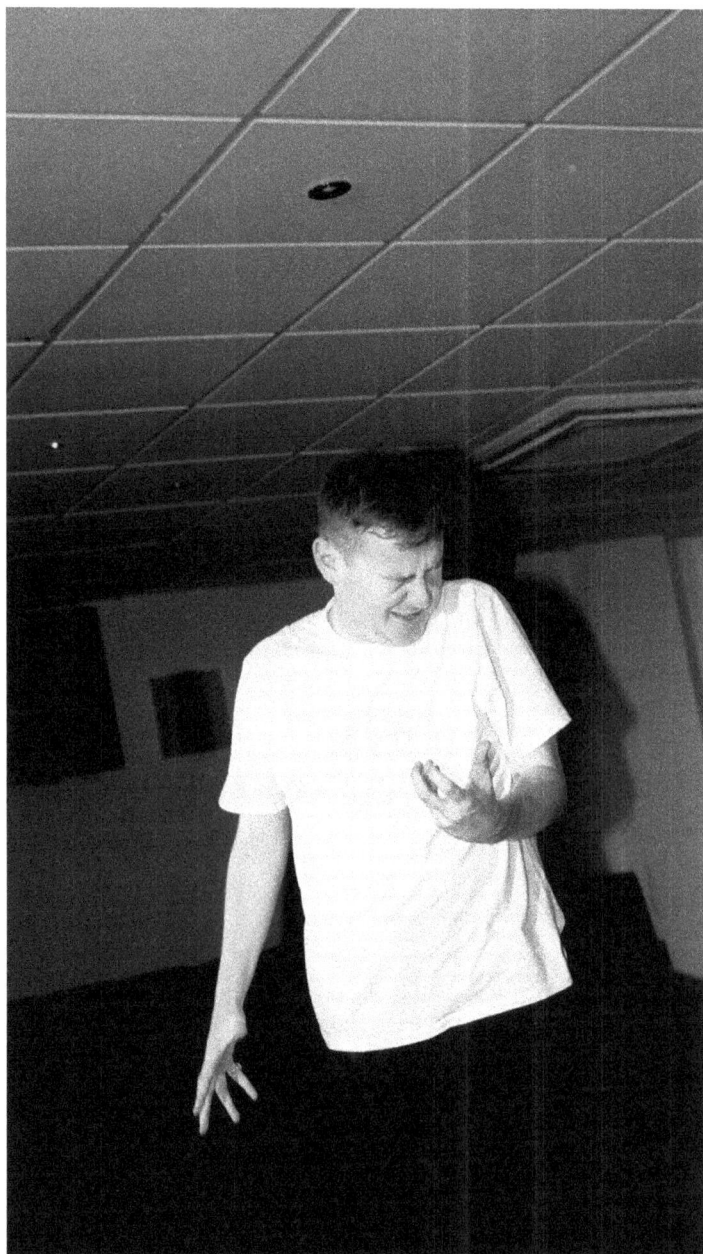

Mark Hannah

Athens of the North

CHARACTERS

ALAN RUTLAND
44 years old, van driver from Gilmerton

LIAM
22 years old, a student at King's College London, from the borders of the East End of London and Essex

MAUREEN
85 years old, originally from Leith but lived most of her life in Edinburgh

NOTES ON PRODUCTION

The original production was performed with only one actor, but feel free to use as many actors as you like.

The original Lothian Regional Transport seating is very rare these days, so it is by no means a necessity. Any seat giving indication of travel should suffice.

This play can be performed in any space.

The action takes place in and throughout the city of Edinburgh across one single day in a contemporary November. This play should have the feeling and the ability to be performed anywhere—in theatres, in social clubs, in the street, on buses. Somewhere where we are among the people of Edinburgh and the spirit is tangible. We should be able to feel the ghosts wherever it may be. The play has been written for one performer and is an episodic monologue, but this is not prescriptive. There is a 1994 original Lothian Regional Transport leather bus seat rooted in place at a 45-degree angle at upstage left. Roots are important here. There is a menu from the Shezan Restaurant resting upright on the seat. Behind the seat, a disposable camera and a lady's handbag rest against it, out of the audience's view.

The PROLOGUE and EPILOGUE of this play should be spoken from a state of neutrality as a narrator and not as a character.

The actor enters the space, standing centre stage.

PROLOGUE

Stone, spires and scenery speak to us,
And we reply, we connect, we forge,
The soundtracks of our lives under Lothian skies,
The old girl's watchful eye on Calton Hill,
These moments of ours are fleeting,
But her eye is eternal,
Voices, shouts, stories, days and nights,
Edina echoing through the ages,
For time shall be the only marker.

A lighting change. The grainy voices of local radio can be heard. Slices of life and news. A small excerpt and it is gone. The sound of static and channel changing fill the space as the voices come and go.

1. THE ANGEL OF ST GILES — ALAN RUTLAND

*ALAN RUTLAND enters, picking up the menu. He is in his early
40s and from Gilmerton. As Edinburgh as they come. He is slightly
hungover, but nothing he hasn't dealt with before. We are in the
Shezan Restaurant on Union Place on an early Sunday evening.*

ALAN: Are you wanting that mixed pakora or jist the
normal yin, Davy?

Nah... cause ah ken you love the one that's got loads eh
the different stuff in it, likesay yir lamb tikka and aw
that. Whit's this yin here?

Mixed Tandoori Grill—a mixture of chicken tikka, seekh
kebab, lamb tikka, sha... shash... something... and king
prawn... aw nut.

Nae fucking chance, naw, you crack on Davy, no fir me
like.

Ya cunt, prawns wae yir Indian is bad enough, no helped
by the fact thiv organised the hail works meal oan a
Sunday and Christ am rougher than a sniper's elbow.
Ended up in The Westie wae John Elliott till fuckin aw
oors last night. Should eh seen me jist there before ye
came in, shakin like fuck tryin tae git the spoon oot the
chutney trays—the tablecloth's like a Jackson Pollock
painting or suhin... aye ken um Davy, the artist boay... did
the big splatter paintings eh... like the Stone Roses and
that, aye, aye!

Of course you've no heard aboot the fuckin trauma fae
last Monday huv ye? Brian cornered me in the warehoose
eh and he says tae me...

BRIAN: Well, it goes without saying, Alan, the orders
arriving and dispatching in the next few days are going
to be much higher than normal, off the scale, so to speak.
So we'll need everybody at the top of their game. But I

am resolutely confident that the company reputation for 'Sound Asleep' will be higher than ever after this week and it'll be a prosperous one for us all, if you, um, catch my drift?

ALAN: Of course, shock horror this roaster wis hanging roond trying tae gie us the company ethos chat. He's the hail reason we've ended up in Shezan at half five on a Sunday picking fae the fucking pre-theatre menu surrounded by everybody gawn over the road to the Playhouse to see *The Lion King* or *The Sound of Music* or whatever pish it is this week.

A la carte? A la cunt mair like.

The lorry delivery boys are brand new tae be fair it's just that arsehole Brian... the cliche machine wae his team building pish and aw that. We deliver mattresses for fucking 'Sound Asleep'... what team building could we possibly need?

It's no been the same since his faither retired, auld Chris. He actually knew wee Kenny aw those years ago believe it or no. He did aye, he was pal's wae Kenny's uncle. What a diamond man. That's sortae why he gie'd me ma first start in here packin the mattresses. Ya cunt it might as well eh been a trampoline centre, mind we used tae lie them oot and bounce between them like it wis a fucking moonlanding. Carnage. But auld Chris just used tae laugh. Eyewis put a score intae yir Christmas caird anaw you mind eh that?

(Beat.)

Ah did you not get that, naw? Hard Lines Davy son, it's tough at the top but it's tougher at the bottom, eh?

Now yiv goat Chris' laddie ower there calling the shots now... it's the smugness aboot him. Christ, Lee Johnson wis a better manager than him. Absolutely sums the cunt up, he's sat across there the now wae a plain naan, a chicken korma and a bottle eh water. Ah kin jist tell it's gonnie be brutal yet again wae the deliveries and the orders and that... that's why he's dragged us aw oot on a Sunday hinkin it'll soften the blow when we're uptae our eyes in it the morn. Well, he's already learned no tae fuck wae Alan Rutland here.

Of course ah hud tae watch, though... wee Erin was dain a performance hing wae her school on the Monday at St Giles Cathedral. Proper big deal like, the Gilmerton Primary School Orchestra performing songs fir sortae the Lord Provost and the council dignitaries and that... nivir hud an orchestra when we were at Gilmerton right enough, Christ imagine that, eh! Me, you and Kenny stood in front eh it like the fuckin Supremes. Well, obviously ah'm Diana Ross, ya cunt.

But aye there's a teacher that runs it, Mrs Blair or suhin, fuck knows ah've nivir met her eh, but apparently oor Erin is a star violin player and got tae do her own wee song as part eh the performance.

She started it up aboot a year ago... the school gied her yin for some initiative or suhin. Well, aye she's at mine on a Monday and a Friday eh... and she's a wee star... but honest tae fuck it wis jist relentless. The first few months it wis jist fingernails doon a blackboard... these wee strings screeching and grinding away aw afternoon right fae me picking her up right, right up until her Ma coming tae get her... ah've been carrying mattresses aboot aw day trying tae chill oot, being sat doon and subjected tae *Twinkle Twinkle Little Star* again and again and again and ah'm tryin tae say tae her 'aye that's magic Erin but you've no learned any DJ Tiesto or Ocean Colour Scene huv ye?'

And... the absolute topper eh it aw... it turned oot that her Ma wis flying oot tae Fuerteventura that morning wae her new guy on the scene... so that left the door wide open fir Dad here and his front seat reserved wae the Councillors. She'd been on the phone aboot it... tryin tae gie us sly digs aboot being a glory hunter and aw the rest eh it.

She wis saying that it starts at twelve sharp... cause that's when the Councillors and Provost are to be formally sat doon or some pish... and she wis saying if ah dinny appear she's talking aboot getting solicitors involved and that cause... jist... ah've been missing child maintenance payments the past few months, eh. It's no ma fault, it's jist a bit tight and folk arenae falling over themselves to buy mattresses the now either so the hours at work are getting cut anaw... so ah dinny ken how Brian's pulling oot aw these orders oot eh naewhere saying aw it's a massive week coming up and that and I'm like aye I git that Brian but wir needing mair than that cause I cannie be in limbo especially wae bairns maintenance payments and that. Ach, fuck knows what he's dain Davy, but ah was just sat there thinking these orders better no fuck me over fir Erin's performance, eh.

So we're aw getting packed away right gawn oot after we've locked up... and ah'm tryin tae catch Brian cause he loves a wee Irish goodbye cause he disnae really drink, see, yiv got tae watch um, he's got mair faces than the Balmoral clock eh, and ah'm saying...

Brian, here eh, Brian, was gonnie double check aboot the schedule that yiv...

BRIAN: Oh Alan! Hello! Deary me that was some day wasn't it? Now, I've booked the Shezan for us all this Sunday, so I'm going to take off... oh but yes Alan, this is Erin's piano thing at St Giles, well, not to worry I've managed to sort it but it will mean double deliveries later in the week, Alan, it's all got to balance out somehow but...

He brings out a piece of folded paper from his back pocket

...it's all sorted!

He tosses it down onto the seat

So you can... sleep soundly on that one!

ALAN cautiously approaches the paper, it will make or break Erin's day.

ALAN: Ah kent the delivery address as soon as ah seen it on the invoice sheet. Peffermill Road... jist doon fae Craigmillar Castle Gardens... right oan the corner. Auld boy here, Ronnie MacIver, he's ordered a Queen-size memory foam, a simple enough wee joab, nice and easy. See... if ah'm anywhere remotely near Peffermill ah'm jist instantly ten yir auld again cause eh wee Kenny's spot, ken? Mind Davy, we would aw muck aboot up there aw the time. It wis a late afternoon, June, last week eh school. Mind Italia 90? Aye, it wis the same day Cameroon were playing the quarter final against Colombia and me and Kenny were oot on the grass at the flats wae this Mitre baw he hud, taking shots and that. This Mitre was fucking stunning, bright orange size five, this hing was as bright as the sun in the sky that day... pure blinded every time ah'm in goals trying tae save it... so he went in goals fir a bit... we jist put our jumpers doon for goals, that was it, eh.

ALAN places the delivery sheet down to mark a goalpost and takes off his overshirt/jumper to mark the other.

And there was this moment where it bounced in front eh me and ah jist caught it right oan the half volley and leathered it right intae the imaginary top corner...

YAAAAAAAAAAAAAAAAAAAAAAAAAAAAAAAAAAAAAAS!

Kenny's gutted like, he wis getting naewhere near that yin, and the baw's rolling aw the way doon the grass, and 'goalie gets it'... that's jist the rule, eh? And he's pelting doon the wee verge and it's bounced off the kerb and he went flying oot... And this van's come hurtling roond the corner... he wis caught in no man's land, he's just ran oot on full momentum eh... ah did, ah did ah shout at him but couldnae even git his full name oot before the very worst sound ah huv ever heard... he wis jist under there... somewhere... and ah mind this woman comin sprinting ower fae the high flats and she's fucking screaming at ey's taking me by the shooders turning me roond telling me no tae look and no tae turn back and keep comin wae her and everything's OK and...

You went tae the funeral eh, Davy? At Mortonhall? Aye my ma says ah was too young and wouldnae let me go, eh. Ah left um there on Peffermill Road under the summer sun. Sound asleep.

ALAN picks the sheet up again with frantic urgency.

See, and ah knew, ah jist fucking knew that selfish prick Brian was gonnie cut it too fine fir time when dain the orders... by the time ah'm finished playin mattress Tetris wae Ronnie MacIver's spare room it wis already half eleven... fuck me this is gonnie be tighter than two coats eh paint man... so ah put the fit doon straight oot eh there gawn the long way back oot cause ah really cannie be dealing wae wee Kenny's spot, jist no on Erin's performance day... and if Brian hus fucked this up he's gittin ma notice, he can barely gie me guaranteed hours as it is... that's whit seventeen years' eh company loyalty gits ye... seventeen fuckin year... that and her fucking solicitor's chat anaw, ah'm only getting Erin oan Mondays and Fridays it's no askin fir much! How kin she no see that?!

Ah'll tell ye something else anaw, these councillors will be gittin it baith barrels when ah get there fir the roadworks and cycle lanes and that. Ah'm huvin' tae come up fuckin Hannover Street then right up the Mound but tae be fair doon the slope at Hannover's a breeze thank Christ and the Mound isnae looking too bad... the wee dash clock in front eh me is saying 11:53, it's gonnie be fine Erin, it's gonnie be golden, Dad's comin tae see you, on the big stage for big stars and at the red light at the top eh the Mound on the corner eh the High Street... there's this mass eh people jist stopping right in front eh the van wae high viz on and big signs and that, they pull oot this massive banner thit says, "JUST STOP OIL" oan it and thir's a few mair who're jist sat right in the middle eh the road. Ah'm watchin the lights go red, amber, green, red, amber, green, red, amber, green...

Whit ur yous fuckin dain ya fuckin idiots?! Move! Move! And thirs horns blasting behind me, the cars are backed up right the way doon the Mound.

AH CANNIE MOVE! AH CANNIE GO ANYWHERE!

11:57 and ah kin fuckin see the front eh St Giles across the way... ah cannie abandon the van it's goat company branding everywhere. Brian would fucking finish me but he's the only reason that ah'm fuckin here!

So ah've jumped oot saying tae them get off the road and they're jist silent... no a word... and ah'm pleading:

Please, ma daughter's over at St Giles jist let me roond the corner, she's performing the day... ah need to see her... please, ye dinny understand, they might take her way fae...

PROTESTOR: THIS IS FOR YOUR DAUGHTER'S FUTURE!

This wee fuckin blue-haired pronoun cunt starts piping up eh, and his/her/their pal does anaw, and no a fuckin Edinburgh accent between any eh them either... dinny you fuckin try it and dinny bother mentioning ma daughter again.

And ah'm slamming the van door ah cannie even speak and the dash clock's saying 11:59 and ah'm jist revving... revving like absolute hell at this crowd eh orange high viz and ah'm ready tae jist fuckin blast them... aw wearing the same orange as wee Kenny's Mitre... and ah'm ready tae blast that shot aw over again, like a 96th minute winner at Easter Road and it's sailing intae the top corner ah'm sorry Kenny ah nivir meant tae hit it that hard you were eyewis better at fitbaw than me and the wheels fae under me are screeching like Wee Erin's violin strings... and there's this one boy at the front... who's stood wae this pure gentle stare... holding this sign...

He looks like a wizard or suhin... white hair and beard wae these proper blue eyes eh... like Kenny but as if he hudnae hud the pause button pushed on him... jist so peaceful... like he's meditating or suhin eh, and the sign says...

DON'T DESTROY YOUR ONLY OPTION!

Ma only option... and there's loads eh noise and the polis are here and... there's bairns. There's bairns coming oot the front eh St Giles in Gilmerton uniforms and ERIN! Erin's at the back eh thum! Fuck the van, that's ma bairn stood there... and ah'm battering o'er the cobbles on the high street eh, still spat on the Heart right enough... fuckin Hearts bastards. Just aboot flattened this English laddie, clattered right intae um oan ma way past, he wis lookin up at fuck knows whit...

Erin! Erin! Ah'm here... ey, ey... am here... and thir aw just shocked... whit is it darling?

There wis too much noise from outside, aw ah know... ah know sweetheart it's OK... they couldn't start it ah know it's noisy oot here isn't it? There's too many people... aw I know, it's yir big moment, it's OK...

And she's greetin.

Let's jist go hame, eh... let's go hame... and the wizard wae Kenny's blue eyes gies her a tissue. He jist came up tae her and handed it tae her and she... smiled.

(Beat.)

Aye... thanks, pal.

And everything jist... vanished. It aw jist wisnae important.

ALAN retreats towards the seat, collapsing into it with a mixture of exhaustion and relief, dropping the delivery sheet onto the floor as he does so.

So wiv went straight hame and ah've turned aw the lights oaf and ah'm thinking... ah'll git ma lighter oot, ken like

Murrayfield or suhin! Lighter oot... set up her wee music stand... she's got the violin tuned up and ready and... ah've nivir seen her look mair grown up. Flame fae ma lighter glowing on this guardian angel.

Right star girl, let's hear it, right fae the start mind... aye the start, how? What did you say?

Aye OK the top then, Christ. One, two, three, aaaaannddd...

Twinkle twinkle, little star...

ALAN begins to sing the song, there is a lighting change and his voice fades into the radio, broadcasting soft instrumental guitar music and more local radio transmissions.

2. LONGING AND LOSING — LIAM

Adjusting himself into the seat is LIAM. A 23-year-old from the borders of London and Essex. He looks small and the nerves are rattling through him. He sits before the Head of Meteorology at Kings' College London. It's a disciplinary matter. His future on the course here hangs in the balance. A disposable camera is held tightly.

I'll be honest I ain't ever been in a proper disciplinary or that. I wanted to start off by genuinely saying sorry. I shouldn't have gone AWOL on exam week.

Cause it was like, the end of first year, I just wanted out for a bit. I love the course, right, but I'd been feeling proper nervous about it all year, I genuinely nearly quit in like Easter, and I can't lie I crawled over the line at the end of first year, and I just needed to breathe and get out for a bit, go and experience some actual proper brilliant weather instead of just analysing maps and formations of it. It was a proper last-minute deal for two hundred quid and I realised... people on my course spend that on one night out. It was a proper lottery obviously... but honestly, that two hundred paid for more than I could ever have hoped for.

See... to begin with I never really fancied myself for the whole lads' holiday abroad type thing. Obviously I drink and stuff and I like travelling and that... but when you like, see them in the airport and that... looking like they've just done a tour of Afghanistan with Burger King shrapnel everywhere, it somehow ain't appealing, you know?

And there was a reason this place was going for two hundred quid at the last minute. They was playing techno at reception at 11 in the morning and the guy who took us to our room didn't blink once during the entire interaction but did however fill us in on his theory that it was the ancient Aztecs who invented WiFi. Zigzagging through the stains in the room which were never one

consistent colour, contrasted with the luminous-coloured
Aftershock and Tequila Rose laying about the place. If
any of them colours started appearing on our weather
maps over in digital analysis... we'd be advising immediate
evacuation for anybody within a 20 mile radius. It was
seriously grim but the saving grace was this Scottish girl
and her mates who'd obviously booked the same crack-den
deal. See I ain't ever been to Scotland but she sounded
proper strange. We was all in the bar across the road, and
me and her, we was doing the dance already though, you
don't even realise it but it just happens, the movements
in the moment, you know? Drinking, looking, looking,
drinking, pretending you need the toilet so you can check
your hair and go for a walk-by, and on the third one...

CHLOE: You'll be oan the Paris flight the morn then, aye?

LIAM: Paris? Uh... no, why?

CHLOE: Aw right... see ah thought you'd be flying straight
tae Paris Fashion Week the amount eh runway walking
you've been dain between here and the toilets... you look
fine eh.

LIAM: I was clearly letting my four Heinekens flow through
me cause out of absolutely nowhere we just lock eyes
out of sheer tension and she's holding me to it she ain't
moving her eyes at all and I'm shitting it now trying to do
anything... suddenly fascinated by how many ornate Greek
floor tiles there are in this absolute monstrosity of a bar
and just as I break the gaze... she starts laughing. Then she
just starts ordering these drinks that have got actual flames
coming out of them... like this guy is actually standing over
them with a lighter and I'm stood with this Scottish girl
who's literally ordered a petrol bomb.

See it's on fire... like the rest of Greece at the moment!

And I knew that chat was gonna get harder cause the
music was gradually getting louder and I doubt that she's
been closely analysing the growing forest fires outside of
Thessaloniki but those Greek flames burned away all the

awkwardness and her name's Chloe and we've broken off from the rest of them stood at the side of this dance-floor bit. She even smells like summer, her hair almost sparkled under the lights, and she goes into her bag and pulls out this disposable camera and just as I'm about to ask why she's got... and FLASH.

LIAM clicks the camera shutter and a flash projects across the audience.

Flirtatious fire becomes permanent on film and the music's playing proper loud now and when I stop seeing stars I realise that she's getting further away and...

Before LIAM can finish, the chorus of 'Who Knows What You'll Find' by Confidence Man begins playing.

I missed last year's holiday cause I was doing the Uni prep. I honestly wasn't sure about it all at the start, it's proper heavy and analytical, I ain't even sure if I'm sure about it now and of course almost right on cue Chloe's asking what it is I do and...

'Who Knows What You'll Find' continues, really kicking into life.

LIAM: I do Meteorology.

CHLOE: WHAT?

LIAM: I said METEOROLOGY!

Nah, nah it ain't nufin to do wiv like asteroids or meteors or that, it's the weather, and she was saying the weather where she's from was awful recently doing this photography portfolio, and this place Cramond in Edinburgh is a statement piece for an area that, if current climate trends continue, will be underwater in a hundred years. Ah that ain't bad I said, if the booze cruise here is shit we can just move it there instead!

She's showing me these other photos on her phone and laughing about our Burgh booze cruise business venture then she... kisses me... there and then and in a particle accelerator of flames, high pressure and heat, the climate graph disintegrates and the glory and zenith of summer youth is projected down the strip, up to the sky and across the Mediterranean in glorious Technicolor.

So... um... what are you doing tomorrow?

CHLOE: Fancy going on a walk, weatherman? I hear the forecast is gid.

LIAM: Fuuuuucking hell.

So the next day we ended up miles from everyone out on some hill. The fire from last night was an inferno, who the fuck climbs a hill in 93% humidity? And that ain't even me being all weather weird, it's just common sense?

LIAM picks up ALAN's goalpost and slings it across his shoulders and back.

We're high enough that we can see the hills on the other islands. Nearly as high as the Greek Gods themselves.

Feels like Athens is right there... as if you could just reach out and touch it.

CHLOE: Aye very good... am fae the real Athens, though.

LIAM: And to be fair you might as well be from Athens cause I still can't understand anyfin you're fuckin sayin'

And she said no... she said...

CHLOE: The Athens of the North.

And I remember when she said that... the sky and oceans all blended... and the forecast was all irrelevant. A Beaufort Scale to measure wind on land and at sea went totally off the scale and into infinite blue. And beyond that blue was one of the greatest cities in the world, one of the cradles of democracy and civilization, but Chloe had toppled absolutely all of it all while still hungover from the night before. Effortless.

Those days after were unbelievable, we didn't even need to strain to hear each other over music any more, we just read each other that well. She came to our room one morning and said she'd booked jetski's later that day, I just totally went with it and that and... everything else, and I ain't really went with anyfin before but with her it was simply enough. Even right up until the fork in the road in the terminal when all my skies led to Stansted... she showed me the camera and it had photos left on it.

CHLOE: Come see the weather in Edinburgh some time, plenty fur you to study that's fir sure.

When I got back here and started second year... we'd been messaging, not a lot but like back and forward and she was asking how it was going and told me how great it is, doing my actual passion and strength... but I just got back into feeling like totally indifferent about it all, just the same dullness to it, like what is the actual point of it? And I was so close to replying and just saying I have no idea what the fuck I'm doing here, it's full of fuckin Roy Croppers, d'you wanna just go back to Zante? Cause I can't be doing wiv all this like pressure and dread... cause that week was ours. That was it. That was the feeling and the moment. The best summer ever.

We were sitting looking at storm data and I was finkin about those people who get in their car and chase tornadoes, right? They certainly ain't meteorologists, they're more like the techno geezer who was on reception... but that summer wasn't sat calculating pressure drops and wind speed... that summer was in the eye of the storm, like releasing my own atmospheric pressures for a bit.

I went straight out of here, down Euston Road, into King's Cross and booked the next train to Edinburgh. Left all my notes and files in that very room across the corridor right there. Just dropped the lot. And yeah that's totally on me for not sending an email to lecturers or pastoral care or that, I was just so consumed by it, and when Chloe had said yeah it'd be great to catch up I really didn't need anyfin else at that stage.

Edinburgh Waverley washed me into a tsunami of sleet and sideways ice and after swimming the winter tide to the taxi rank...

Hello, sorry, I ain't looking for a fare but do you know where COCK-BURN Street is? Yeah, yeah COCK-BURN

Ahhhhhh Co-Burn!

I was surrounded by stone going up that Royal Mile. The castle in the distance was mine, like I'd been victorious in some foreign conquest and now the princess was welcoming me home from battle. It was like she was the warm weather front of sunshine against the Scottish greyness. I was so busy looking up at it all... and then this guy smashed into me right there, yeah he was sprinting towards that cathedral church thing. Maybe he'd had divine intervention or something I dunno. The speed he whacked me at, his own guardian angel must have materialised on the altar. I remember thinking wow, how unreal it must be to have that level of faith in something, well in anything, really.

CHLOE: Liam, Zante was unreal, and it's so great to see that you actually came... I genuinely didn't think you would. I have a boyfriend, and I really don't think this will eh... yeah.

LIAM: And that was that. Smashed into a million bits. I dunno why I never even saw it coming, then I'm obviously going... what the fuck am I doing? Missing my second-year exams to just disappear to a city I've never even been to and when she said it I only realised... for a girl I never really actually knew, either.

Nobody even knows where I am.

I don't even know where I am.

Why was I even bothering with any of it? With all of it? All that time, that effort... the scholarship. Fuck. But I walked and walked away as far as I could away from the storms and the thundering rain of my own delusions and I came to this little river or summink. These big, sweeping crescents and cobbles and white street lights... it was like Disney or a storybook or... Stockbridge.

Sat by this stream just watching the water. Everything flows. No science to it, no calculation, no measurement, it is because... it just is.

Imagine that though, "Liam why did you abandon all your upcoming examinations, progress and academic potential? Went up to some mad gaff, got lost among loads of tourists and looked at some water."

Fuck me... could have just gone down to the Thames.

When I got on the bus to go to the station, it was amazing how different the main bit was just a couple of hours later... the city was so cold and so clear. Unbelievable.

LIAM stands upstage right, looking across at the seat.

But there was this woman on the top deck of the bus when I was near the station and she just kept talking away to herself, she was like laughing one minute and ranting away like a lunatic the next. I couldn't understand cause we was the only two people upstairs at that time of night and it took everything left in me to, to ask her... are you alright? And she started it all up again with all these different names and all she did was start shouting... fuck knows... could have done with the little bus tracker screen having subtitles running alongside it... and I just sprinted off. I couldn't, you know, I was trying to help her but there was nothing left in me by that stage. And I was under that big hotel clock thing for ages freezing.

Chloe was saying that clock tower is always five minutes fast so people don't miss their trains. I thought that was genius, so I just stood there for exactly five minutes, watching it all one last time. I stood under the clock with her camera. It had one photo left on it. It started with us but it ends with all... this. She said she'll see me on the tele doing the weather and that I was the smartest person she's ever met... still not sure what to do with that. In a city of spires and palaces for that ephemeral beat of high pressure on a Scottish soundtracked heatwave she truly was The Queen. Stood looking out at Edinburgh, those buildings that have stood for hundreds of years in all weathers, more weathers than we could ever analyse or chart or anyfin, beauty being broken then rebuilt all around me... watching it all sparkle through a plastic lens.

I'll take any disciplinary stuff or anyfin like that, cause obviously in that moment I was wrong and weren't finkin and yeah you can predict and forecast all you want and you can sit there with the graphs and percentages but when there's a freak heatwave, you go to it. Chasing the summer, innit? So yeah, fuck it, I'd do it all again in a heartbeat. Just for that view at night time, one more time, any time. But that's also why I'd uh... I'd love the chance to sit the modules properly, no nonsense or that. That view brought it all into focus, you know? But I will stand in Stockbridge again... in the summer. And that'll be the final click on the film.

A beat. He may just have swung this. Just.

If we're done, I've got an appointment like right now to get these developed, so...

LIAM, at peace with it all now, puts the camera down and begins to retreat, a million miles away from Zante, a million miles from this office in central London with his heart and mind firmly in Edinburgh. He begins to shift. 'To Grow' by Swim School plays, followed by more radio broadcasts.

3. WANDERING UNDER THE STARS - MAUREEN

There is another lighting change. MAUREEN comes into place on the seat with a sense of ownership. She is in her mid-80s and an old Leither. She brings a single cigarette from her pocket and stands downstage centre.

MAUREEN: Aye! Aye! Ah've been telt huv ah? Telt aboot it when, son? Ah'm jist huvin a fag the now... ye nivir telt me ah hud tae go ootside... naw when wis that? Ach ah don't know... naw ye urnae comin wae me ah kin dae it masel... you better no be asking me oot, Ross! ih-hih, exactly! Aw Ross you're the best eh us, son... nivir oot eh here making sure we're awright. You're the only yin that ah kin remember right enough... and yir awfy handsome, very tall... yir a, a, a gay laddie, are ye no? Bloody keep huvin tae remind me there wis a smoking ban or something... but ah seen ye wae your Benson and Hedges ootside, aye, caught red-handed one morning oot the front didn't ah, and ye mind what ye said aye?

ROSS: Ugh, it's absolutely brutal, eh, Maureen? Nae fags inside?! Clearly ah nivir goat the fuckin memo!

MAUREEN: Aye! Aw we do have a laugh, don't we, son? It wis ma laddie Peter whae pit me in here. See apparently ah'm no very well, and thir saying ah'm no allowed to stay in the hoose anymair... but like ah keep saying tae them there's nothing wrong wae me aye exactly there's nothing wrong wae me at aw. Ah got overruled, yit again, that's how ah've landed in here, eh. Peter wis saying awwwww yir struggling... well he jist aboot got a fucking slap fir his cheek ah tell ye... imagine that eh, yir ain mother. He says ah wis gawn oot tae the shops but then coming back wae nothing. Ah says naw... ma messages are aw here son and ah went tae open the fridge door and there wis nothing but a light and a draft. Ah couldnae understand... ah pit them away masel... he watched me dae it! Obviously no. And then he says when ah did manage tae git the messages ah wis leavin thum everywhere! Oh aye, apparently ah wis on the front step wae Jean fae next door, littering her lobby wae milk, bread, cat food... ah've no even got a fuckin cat, and Peter found out aboot it, aye that wis awfae gid eh you tae grass me in, Jean eh... ya backstabbing bitch.

So that wis me... carted intae here. 'West Edinburgh Residential Care'... am miles away fae the bloody hoose. That Peter disnae half make an arse eh it sometimes, ah says tae um... that's minimum two buses in the mornings that's gonnie be ridiculous and he says 'it's fine Mum you dont have to worry aboot the hoose any mair ah've taken care eh it.' Ah says what are ye talkin aboot cause he thinks am fucking daft but clear as day, clear as bloody day, ah remember aw the boxes in the living room and the kitchen wis aw bare and Peter's sayin tae me 'yir gonnie be living in a new house now Mum... but it's a special house where people yir ain age'll be there.' Ah hud nae idea what he meant, there's nothing wrong wae the hoose ah was in. Me and Alec, his faither, we lived in that hoose 60 odd year... and now thir practically shoving me oot the door! Ah says tae Peter, if your faither wis here he'd fuckin belt ye one. They even hud the new folk movin in oot on the step wae the keys and the papers and that... some young laddie, no much older thin yirsel Ross... and ye want tae eh seen the fuckin state eh um... bloody half-mast troosers, yellae framed glesses and an earring... didnae even look at me... wis jist stood taking photaes on his phone, something aboot the 'look' eh the place, and ah says tae um, you dinny get too comfortable son cause once ah've sorted this oot wae Peter you'll be oot, you'll be fuckin' oot ya... and we wir away, that was it.

They tried tae gie me the flat upstairs, ah says tae thum naw will ah fuck be in the yin up the stair, too high fur me aye, aye, Christ... ah git dizzy wae two pairs eh socks oan. Ma room's aw the wrong way roond, Ross. The chest eh drawers are too far over, the bed's no in the right angle

and they've punted off aw ma stuff, maist eh the stuff
fae the hoose is away.

Ah do huv however, huv ma favourite photae eh me and
Alec... somewhere. Doon in Brighton, right on the pier,
it wis a rare trip that... 1972... sun wis blazing, pier wis
rammed... see Alec eyewis fancied himsel as a bit eh a
Mod so naturally he wis in his element... seagulls swooping
doon on wir chips like fuckin' Stuka divebombers,
ah'm whacking them wae ma bag, Alec's screaming and
shouting, ma loose change is spillin everywhere like a
poor-oot, aw we wir poorless. He'll tell ye himsel, he'll
be here the now, he's eyewis runnin late ye kin whit he's
like. Ah dinny even ken where the rest eh the stuff's aw
went. It'll be ma Peter, ah'm tellin ye. Ah wouldnae ken,
he's oot in Australia the now. Hoose away, mother away,
holiday sorted, and that's him. Ah dinny ken where he got
that selfish bastard syndrome fae... it certainly wisnae me
or his faither.

They other nurses keep telling me they dinny ken how
long it'll be. But like ah keep sayin tae thum there's
nothing wrong wae me at aw. Thir aw jist jealous... that's
whit it is... huvin everything in order and they cannie
hack it. Well, jist like ah says, once ah'm back oot eh here
wae ma hoose sorted and in order they'll aw be regretting
it then, eh.

And mind Ross, you're the absolute best eh us, son. Yir a
diamond.

The nights are the worst. Jist silence. Wir aw jist lying in
the dark waiting tae forget everything and start a new
day aw over again, like taking oor tapes and wiping them
wae lightning. And it's like thirs shadows in ma room,
long dark hings climbing up the waws and dripping doon
thum. And ah'm drifting, jist drifting away and one eh
them is getting closer. It's loomin, stood ower the bed...
ah... Alec...

Alec! Christ they're yir there, ah'v been waiting fur ages! Where have ye been? Ah wis saying to Ross thit yir eyewis late, ah tried tae get um tae stay so you could see um, what is it yiv been dain?

"Looking eftir you," he says, wae a smile as wide as the day ah met him.

It was oor Peter whae put ey's in here.

And it's as if he's no looking directly it me bit looking through me, like he kens the answers before ah've even spoke. He's stood over at the windae.

Awfae dark ootside.

"Let's go," he says.

ALEC: Wir no steyin here... come on Maureen, wir gawn hame.

MAUREEN: Hame?... Aw that sounds rer Alec, aw that sounds awfae gid.

MAUREEN puts her cigarette down starts to put on the overshirt and collect her bag.

He says, "Dinny bring anything else... yir no needing anything. Come oan, let's get shifting."

In a last-minute grab, hoping not to be caught in the act, she picks the cigarette back up.

Yir no wrong Alec eh, it's awfy Baltic... wir gonnie get a bus intae the toon, aye?

You mind eh that day oot in... ah cannie mind... wis it Brighton? Ye mind eh... the chips and ye dropped them... and ah hink there wis a bird or, aye... aye... but he disnae answer, he silently jist waits for the bus... but when wir oan it wir roaring and laughing... sat up the top deck and the toons looking awfy braw the night, aw lit up, right the way doon Princes Street. Wir getting oaf and there's this young laddie, ken a sort eh... an English laddie... awfy handsome, and he's askin me if am awright... eh of course ah'm awright Peter... me and yir faither are gawn intae the toon then wir gawn back tae the hoose so whit dae ye make eh that, eh?! Ye eyewis were a selfish wee bastard you!...and he's off the bus and away over tae Waverley Steps. Aye that'll fucking teach um, eh.

Princes Street's looking awfy well turned oot, shoap fronts are aw gleaming, got their covers oot like when we wir younger wae the auld faces aw there. Willie fae the Evening News stand is chatting tae Alec and the Castle's aw lit up...thirs stars over the Old Town and ah hink that wis where ma ain gran stayed, likesay on the Closes on the High Street. Edinburgh's a village, eh. And in villages everybody kens everybody, whether ye like it or no. Villages dinnae normally huv castles and parliaments and palaces, right enough. And jist when ah says palace, there's this stocky man wae a wee mustache walking by, his shirts soaked through wae blood, punctures aw through his body, but he's walking perfectly straight, wae this big sort eh stride.

Christ what's happened tae you son, are ye awright?

"British bullets," he says, aw defiant, and marches away oor North Bridge heading fur the Cowgate, looking like he could lead an army.

The stack eh Evening News papers is fluttering wae the breeze and the date oan the front eh thum says... Friday the 17th eh November 1972... and the back says **TURNBULL'S TORNADOES CAUSE A STORM** and it's Jimmy O'Rourke, Eric Schaedler and the King... Pat Stanton. Here Alec, Alec, ye mind eh that time in Brighton, naw, naw, Blackpool... aye Blackpool wae the pigeon aye and you eyewis wanted tae be a Mod mind!

And he's aw blunt "it wisnae Brighton. And it wisnae a seagull."

And when he says it, ye cannie see his breath in the air, there's jist nothing. Alec... why are ye in jist a shirt are ye no freezing? Ah'm no that daft... Alec where's yir jaiket? Are you sure yir awright, Alec?

He says, "Dinny worry aboot me, ah'm the same as ever."

Thiv started smashing doon the tenements at St James' Square... thir saying it's gonnie be aw shoaps soon in there apparently, awfy shame, Leith Street's gonnie feel that yin, aye. The Drummonds used tae stay in that corner yin aye, ye mind eh Tam, eh Alec? Used tae work at Scottish and Newcastle. And the Rae's, they wir through the waw fae them. Aye, Hugh Rae. Mind they ey used tae caw um Hip Hip. Aye! Hip Hip Hugh Rae!

This pair eh Yanks are stood talking aboot some AirBnB code for the door asking if this is Leith. Naw that's the Port, that's the Port yir wantin tae be in. This is Leith Street. This is the toon. This is ma toon. And eh dinny be hinkin ye kin just be helpin yirsel tae number 34 either, cause we're gid pals wae the Drummonds.

Alec's telling me that ah need tae hurry up but am cauld, am cauld Alec, am chittering, mibbie we should go back, wiv come too far... ah dinny like this any mair Alec ah dinny think we should be oot this late, wee Ross will be wondering where ah am.

Alec's saying it's awright he's got the heating on in the hoose... huv ye been back? And the heating's on aye?

And aw he says is, "Ah've been there the hail time."

The Picture Hoose just doon fae the Playhoose is glowing in the dark... aw Alec look, look, thir showing *The 3:10 tae Yuma*, and it's a double feature wae *The Gunfight at The O.K Corral*! Aw come oan let's go eh, ye eyewis loved the Westerns and Burt Lancaster and that, come oan it'll be starting jist now but he keeps saying naw, we've no goat time and ah says but wiv no been fir years, we'll still git the first five minutes eh it and he's telling me that's enough...but ah want tae go will ye jist let me go... stop it, stop now and it's... it's him again, him again, him that wis in Brighton wae the hammer, whae came for ma purse fae behind, and ah was whackin um, ah wis, Alec it's him, it's fuckin him, that thieving bastart that wis grabbing me, whit are ye dain, Alec? You're the boy in Brighton! Ye are! Dinny try it wae me! Try raising yir hands again tae me Alec Purves!

MAUREEN raises her hands with aggression but is scared and cowers defensively on the floor. She then adjusts her arms and rounds them into an embrace.

ALEC: Sssshhhhhh, ey, ey, ssshhhhh naw Maureen naw, ah sorted him out. He wis an auld lunatic, jist tryin his luck, Christ, that wis years and years ago, that wisnae in Brighton, that wis Portabellae, can you no remember?

Silence.

MAUREEN: And he holds me. Bringing his airm up and he's telling me tae lead the way doon Elm Row.

MAUREEN releases from the embrace. Her fag-holding hand gently stretches out, the cigarette itself upright, as if lighting the way.

The clock's lit up... a guardian angel, oor true north star... and it's as if wir floating, gliding doon the top eh Leith Walk, Alec's laid oot a magic cairpet fir us both, it's aw so easy, nae effort, it's numb kind eh... breezing wir way way intae Annandale Street, and by sain nothing... wir sayin everything.

The street's silent. The moon glowing down ontae the road. And am so, so cauld and Alec's gittin distant, he's still there but he's getting blurry, like the signal's away or suhin... jist stood over the road wae that stare, as if he's lookin through me again.

The radio sound creeps back into life momentarily, playing the chorus of 'Lady Willpower' by Gary Puckett and The Union Gap.

That was what we eyewis used tae sing but he's jist standing looking over at number 58... at the hoose.

Wir here... and aww it looks jist marvellous.

Thanks for bringing me hame, Alec.

ALEC: Bringing *us* hame, Maureen

MAUREEN: Alec... why did ye come and git me?

ALEC: You'll ken. Souls eyewis belong somewhere... and this is where oors belong... right here.

MAUREEN: Ah'm frozen. Alec's so faint, noo. He's almost whispering.

ALEC: Welcome hame, hen, dinny worry the heating's on... ye nivir telt me it wis nine fuckin grand tae pit the heating oan right enough... but ah'll be waiting... am the dust that blows along the road. You'll feel me.

MAUREEN: The columns on Calton Hill look tiny fae here. The plinths eh the Gods on the mountain. Blue lights are flashing off the hooses and the ice under me feels like it's melting... Alec... Alec... where are ye? Ah'm lookin fur Alec, huv ye seen him anywhere? I need Alec, where is he? Jean fae next door is oot and thir aw roond me and Ross... aw Ross... am sorry son, am really sorry.

Ah'm looking up and the stars over the toon are like wee lanterns in the blackness... infinite light, spirits powering them forever and ever, and now... there'll be one mair twinkling over Edinburgh... everything we were, everything we are and everything wir yet tae become... eh.

She gazes to the skies. The cigarette in hand is gently crushed into ash and dust. MAUREEN slowly ebbs away. Away from the audience, away from Edinburgh, into the stars of the November night and into history.

The actor re-emerges and places the handbag down on the seat. They return to stand centre stage as music begins to play.

EPILOGUE

Stone, spires and scenery speak to us,

And we reply, we connect, we forge,

The soundtracks of our lives under Lothian skies,

The old girl's watchful eye on Calton Hill,

These moments of ours are fleeting,

But her eye is eternal,

Voices, shouts, stories, days and nights,

Edina echoing through the ages,

For time shall be the only marker.

   Blackout.

END.

ALSO AVAILABLE FROM SALAMANDER STREET

All Salamander Street plays can be bought in bulk at a discount for performance or study. Contact info@salamanderstreet.com to enquire about performance licenses.

A PLAY, A PIE AND A PINT: VOLUME TWO
8 One-Act Plays from Òran Mór.
ISBN: 9781068696237

To celebrate the beloved Glasow theatrical institution's 20th anniversary, this second collection includes critically acclaimed plays and favourites as voted by the public and members of the theatre company.

PLACEHOLDER by Catherine Bisset
ISBN: 9781068696282

A parallel text version of Catherine Bisset's dramatic solo play set in 1790 Saint-Domingue – the daughter of an enslaved woman reflects on her life as an opera singer and the importance of resistance.

THE CHING ROOM & TURBO FOLK
by Alan Bissett
ISBN: 9781913630997

A pitch-black two-hander set in a toilet cubicle, and a sharp look at Scottish nationality at home and abroad.

GROUP PORTRAIT IN A SUMMER LANDSCAPE
by Peter Arnott
ISBN: 9781914228933

An intense and riveting play set in a Perthshire country house during the Scottish Independence referendum of 2014. A retired academic and political heavyweight invites family and former students together for a dramatic reckoning.

O IS FOR HOOLET by Ishbel McFarlane
ISBN: 9781913630126

A solo show about the Scots language that challenges and disrupts our expectations and prejudices about language.